THE MICROSCOPIC WORLD

Viruses

Under the Microscope

By Simon Pierce

Cavendish
Square

Published in 2024 by Cavendish Square Publishing, LLC
2544 Clinton Street Buffalo, NY 14224

Website: cavendishsq.com

This publication represents the opinions and views of the author based on their personal experience, knowledge, and research. The information in this book serves as a general guide only. The author and publisher have used their best efforts in preparing this book and disclaim liability rising directly or indirectly from the use and application of this book.

Disclaimer: Portions of this work were originally authored by John Shea and published as *Viruses Up Close* (Under the Microscope). All new material this edition authored by Simon Pierce.

All websites were available and accurate when this book was sent to press.

Library of Congress Cataloging-in-Publication Data

Names: Pierce, Simon, author.
Title: Viruses under the microscope / Simon Pierce.
Description: Buffalo, NY : Cavendish Square Publishing, [2024] | Series: The inside guide. The microscopic world | Includes bibliographical references and index.
Identifiers: LCCN 2022060722 | ISBN 9781502668028 (library binding) | ISBN 9781502668011 (paperback) | ISBN 9781502668035 (ebook)
Subjects: LCSH: Viruses–Juvenile literature. | Microscopy–Juvenile literature.
Classification: LCC QR365 .P54 2024 | DDC 579.2–dc23/eng/20221222
LC record available at https://lccn.loc.gov/2022060722

Editor: Jennifer Lombardo
Copyeditor: Danielle Haynes
Designer: Deanna Paternostro

The photographs in this book are used by permission and through the courtesy of: Cover creativeneko/Shutterstock.com; p. 4 Bussakan Punlerdmatee/Shutterstock.com; p. 6 bissig/Shutterstock.com; p. 7 (main) Ernsts/Wikimedia Commons; p. 7 (inset) Stanislav Stradnic/Shutterstock.com; p. 10 Relight Motion/Shutterstock.com; p. 13 grayjay/Shutterstock.com; p. 15 Milles Vector Studio/Shutterstock.com; pp. 16, 18 Designua/Shutterstock.com; p. 20 DAntes Design/Shutterstock.com; pp. 22, 27 Pixel-Shot/Shutterstock.com; p. 24 Dalibor Sevaljevic/Shutterstock.com; p. 25 shamiss/Shutterstock.com; p. 28 (top) Yuganov Konstantin/Shutterstock.com; p. 28 (bottom) Christoph Burgstedt/Shutterstock.com; p. 29 (top) nobeastsofierce/Shutterstock.com; p. 29 (bottom) DC Studio/Shutterstock.com.

Some of the images in this book illustrate individuals who are models. The depictions do not imply actual situations or events.

CPSIA compliance information: Batch #CSCSQ24: For further information contact Cavendish Square Publishing LLC at 1-877-980-4450.

Printed in the United States of America

Find us on

CONTENTS

The tobacco mosaic virus causes a pattern of brown splotches to appear on the leaves of the tobacco plant.

DISCOVERING VIRUSES

Viruses existed for billions of years before humans appeared on the planet, yet we didn't know about them until the 19th century. In 1887, a scientist named Dmitry Ivanovsky began studying tobacco mosaic disease, which was killing tobacco plants in the Netherlands. Ivanovsky learned that if he put the sap from a diseased plant into a healthy one, the healthy plant would also become diseased. This showed that there was something **infectious** causing the disease.

At this point in history, people knew about bacteria and were starting to get an idea of how they spread disease. Using special tools, Ivanovsky proved that something even smaller than a bacterium was causing tobacco mosaic disease. However, without the high-powered microscopes that we have today, Ivanovsky couldn't see the virus that was responsible for the disease. It wasn't until the mid-20th century that scientists were able to finally see the tobacco mosaic virus.

> **Fast Fact**
> Just about every form of life on Earth can be attacked by viruses. There are viruses that affect plants, animals, humans, and even bacteria.

Dmitry Ivanovsky is celebrated as the "father of virology," or the study of viruses.

Fast Fact

Many viruses can't be passed between animals and humans. The ones that can are called zoonotic viruses. The virus that causes COVID-19 is one example of a zoonotic virus.

Learning More

In 1898, further evidence appeared that unseen substances other than bacteria could cause disease. Scientist Friedrich Löffler and Dr. Paul Frosch studied the causes of foot-and-mouth disease,

a serious and deadly illness that affects farm animals. Similar to Ivanovsky, the team used filters to show that something much smaller than bacteria could spread foot-and-mouth disease among animals.

Despite these discoveries, some people didn't believe

Under a microscope, scientists can see what viruses, such as the one shown below, look like. This helps them figure out how to fight each virus.

a)

germs smaller than bacteria had anything to do with human diseases. Convincing proof came in 1900, presented by a group of scientists that included U.S. Army doctor Walter Reed. The group was researching yellow fever, an often-deadly disease marked by a high fever. They showed that yellow fever was caused by a germ that could pass through filters that stopped bacteria.

When Germans Max Knoll and Ernst Ruska invented the transmission electron microscope (TEM) around 1931, a powerful new tool became available to help people understand what viruses are and how they behave. Ernst's brother, Dr. Helmut Ruska, was one of the first people to use the TEM to see a virus and study its structure. As scientists got better at using the TEM, they developed a fuller understanding of what a virus is made of and how it causes diseases.

Electron and Optical Microscopes

Optical microscopes use light and special lenses to magnify objects. Electron microscopes bounce electrons—particles with a negative charge—off objects to produce an image. Electron microscopes can magnify things many more times than most optical microscopes, but they can't look at moving objects.

Fast Fact

In addition to proving the existence of the yellow fever virus, Walter Reed and James Carroll showed that the disease was spread by the bite of a mosquito. They proved this when Carroll was bitten by a mosquito that fed first on infected patients!

IMPORTANT FIGURES IN GERM THEORY

Germ theory is the idea that microscopic creatures called microorganisms—also known as germs—cause disease. When scientists first proposed this theory, many people thought the idea of invisible, or unseen, creatures floating through the air was foolish. Thanks to scientists such as Joseph Lister, Robert Koch, and Louis Pasteur, we now know it's true.

Lister was the first person to suggest that doctors wash their hands and **sterilize** their tools before and after surgery. Koch studied microorganisms and figured out which ones caused certain diseases. Pasteur greatly reduced the number of illnesses that are spread through food by implementing a process of heating the food to kill the germs in it—a process we now call pasteurization.

In 2011, a group of scientists in England started using an optical microscope called the microsphere nanoscope. It's powerful enough to see a virus attacking a cell, and since it's an optical microscope, scientists can watch this happen in real time. As scientific instruments continue to improve, we'll likely learn a lot more about the world around us—and our own bodies.

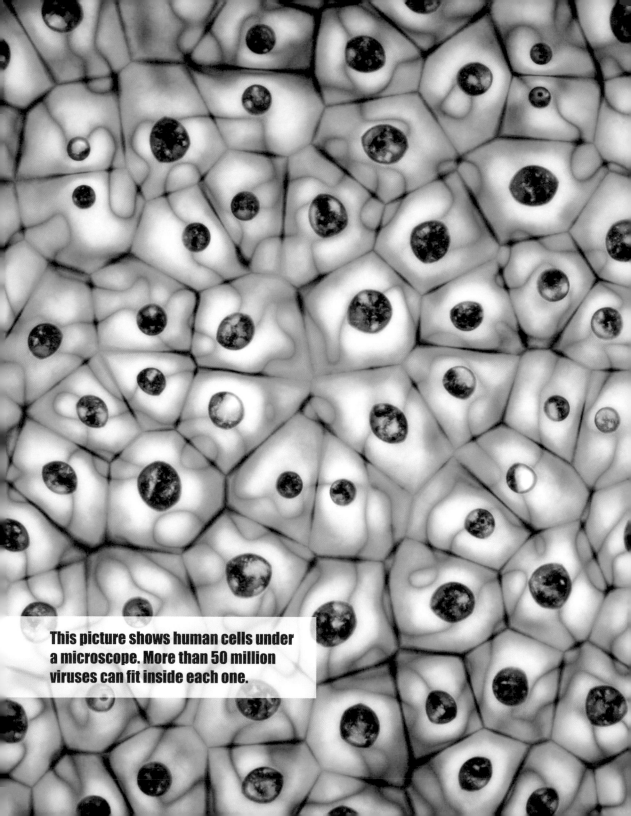

This picture shows human cells under a microscope. More than 50 million viruses can fit inside each one.

TINY GERMS

Viruses are some of the smallest things we know of on Earth. Most range in size from 20 to 300 nanometers. (There are 10 million nanometers in a centimeter.) In comparison, the smallest human cells are about 10,000 nanometers around. This size is difficult to imagine, but consider that over 50 million virus particles can fit into a single human cell!

Until 2003, scientists thought all viruses were this small. However, in the 21st century, larger viruses have been discovered. In 2011, a 700-nanometer virus—named the Megavirus because of its size—was discovered off the coast of Chile. Since then, other large viruses have also been discovered. However, "large" is always a relative term when it comes to viruses. Even the largest ones can still be seen only with a microscope.

Virus Structure

All viruses are made up of at least two parts: **nucleic acid** and a capsid. The capsid is a shell made of **proteins** that surrounds the nucleic acid in a virus. Just like the surface of a soccer ball is made up of smaller shapes that fit together, a capsid is made up of small, repeating shapes that give the virus its larger overall structure. These shapes help them attach to cells.

CLIMATE CHANGE AND VIRUSES

In 2014, scientists thawed, or unfroze, a virus that had been frozen for thousands of years almost 100 feet (30 meters) underground in Siberia, Russia. When it thawed, it was still infectious. However, this virus—which is about 100 times larger than most other viruses—only infects small creatures called amoebae.

Although *Pithovirus sibericum*, as scientists named it, can't infect humans, its recovery raises questions about other viruses that might be frozen. As climate change melts the ice in places such as Antarctica and the Arctic, some people worry that a more dangerous virus might be released.

The innermost part of the virus contains nucleic acid. Nucleic acid is made from molecules called **nucleotides**. Nucleotides attach to one another like beads on a string. The order of the nucleotides forms a code, just like the order of letters in a book forms words and sentences. All life on this planet uses this code to grow and make copies of itself.

Fast Fact

Nucleic acid got its name because scientists first found it in the nucleus of living cells. However, it's been found in things without a nucleus, including bacteria and viruses.

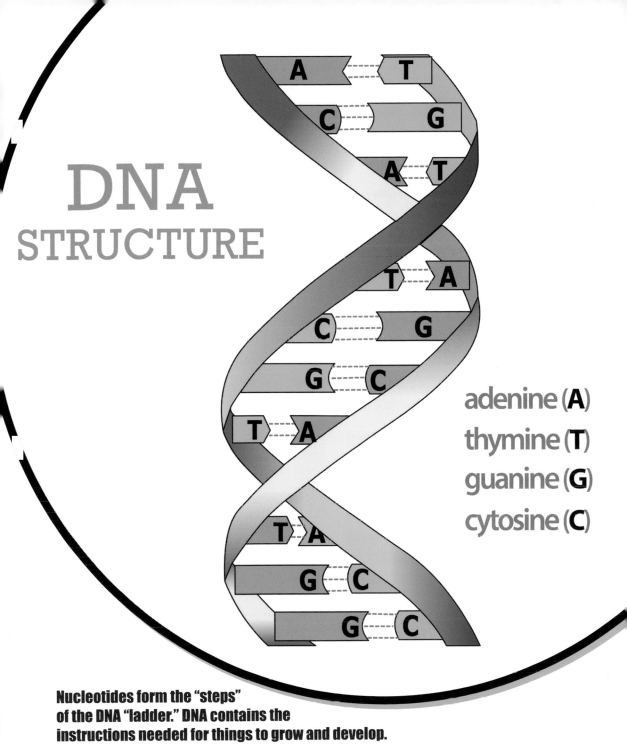

DNA
STRUCTURE

adenine **(A)**
thymine **(T)**
guanine **(G)**
cytosine **(C)**

**Nucleotides form the "steps"
of the DNA "ladder." DNA contains the
instructions needed for things to grow and develop.**

The two types of nucleic acid found in nature are deoxyribonucleic acid (DNA) and ribonucleic acid (RNA). Unlike most living things, which contain both DNA and RNA, viruses contain only one or the other. The nucleic acid in a virus contains the instructions needed to make copies of that virus's parts, including more nucleic acid.

An Extra Feature

In addition to the capsid and nucleic acid, some viruses also have what's called an envelope around the capsid. It's made of proteins and **lipids**. The instructions to make proteins are stored in the nucleic acid. However, a virus doesn't contain any information about how to make the lipids of the envelope. It doesn't need to. The virus steals part of the membrane of the cell it attacks. Many viruses also grow spikes on their envelopes that help them attach to cell surfaces. These are called spike proteins.

Influenza Virus

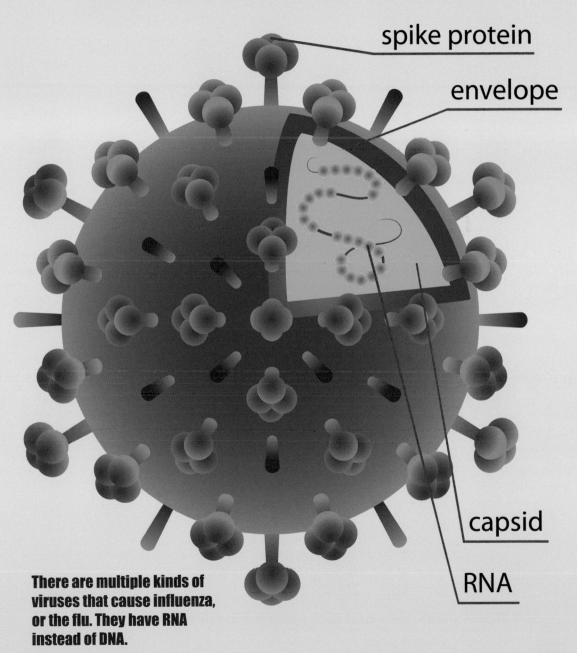

spike protein

envelope

capsid

RNA

There are multiple kinds of viruses that cause influenza, or the flu. They have RNA instead of DNA.

LIFE CYCLE OF VIRUSES

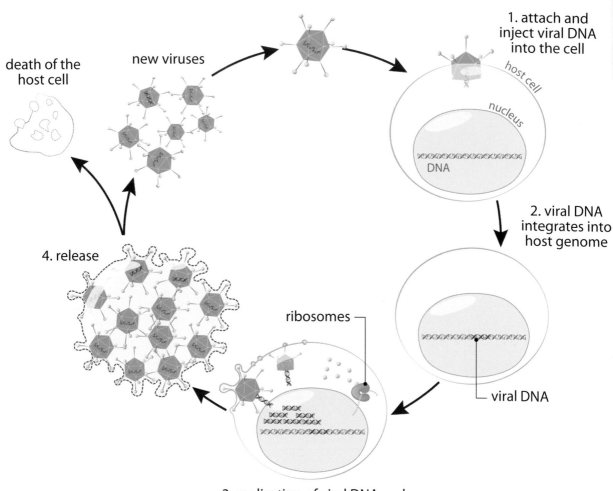

death of the host cell

new viruses

1. attach and inject viral DNA into the cell

host cell

nucleus

DNA

2. viral DNA integrates into host genome

4. release

ribosomes

viral DNA

3. replication of viral DNA and synthesis of viral proteins

This picture shows how a virus uses a host cell to reproduce.

HOW VIRUSES WORK

Viruses are **parasites**. They depend on living cells to make copies of, or replicate, themselves. The virus provides the cell with instructions in the form of nucleic acid, while the cell provides the energy and the building material. Unfortunately, the virus often harms the cell as it replicates.

A virus follows a process to replicate itself. First, it finds a suitable host cell. In the step called adsorption, the virus attaches itself to the outer surface of the host cell. In the next step, called penetration, the virus's nucleic acid gets past the membrane of the host cell. In some cases, the virus's envelope allows it to slide through the membrane. In other cases, the virus tricks the cell into creating an opening to allow the virus to enter. Once inside its host cell, a virus takes control and directs the cell to make more copies of its proteins and nucleic acid.

Entering the Cell

Human cells have special molecules called receptors on their outside

Fast Fact
Viruses that don't have an envelope are called "naked."

VIRAL SHAPES

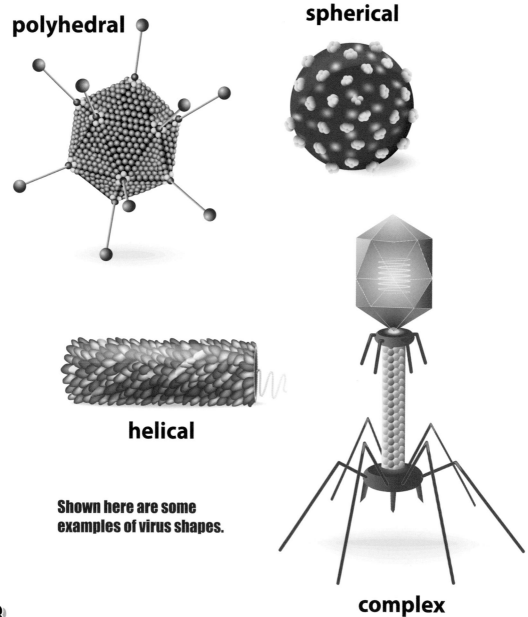

polyhedral

spherical

helical

Shown here are some
examples of virus shapes.

complex

ALIVE OR NOT?

Scientists aren't entirely sure if viruses should be considered alive or not. Most have decided to put them in the "nonliving" category. Living things have DNA, cells, the ability to reproduce, the ability to change over time, and the ability to use energy.

While viruses share much in common with living organisms, they're missing much of the cellular machinery that some scientists insist is needed for something to be considered alive. Viruses have DNA and do change over time, but they can't reproduce by themselves, they don't have cells, and they don't produce energy to use.

Fast Fact

Viruses reproduce so quickly that they sometimes make mistakes when they're copying their genetic material. These mistakes are called mutations. Once a virus has mutated, the body often needs to be retaught how to fight it.

membrane that help cells communicate and interact with each other. Viruses often use these receptors to their benefit. Proteins on either the capsid or envelope (if the virus has one) turn on receptors, much like a key opens a lock. This sparks a process in which the cell brings the receptor inside itself—along with the attached virus.

The next step is the assembly phase. Viral proteins move into a certain area of the cell. There, capsid shells are built around the newly made viral nucleic acid. More than 10,000 new virus particles can be made in a host cell that was infected with just one virus!

Exiting the Cell

Viruses have different ways of exiting the host cell. The most common way for naked viruses to exit is to burst open the cell

This picture shows how viruses damage a cell when they exit.

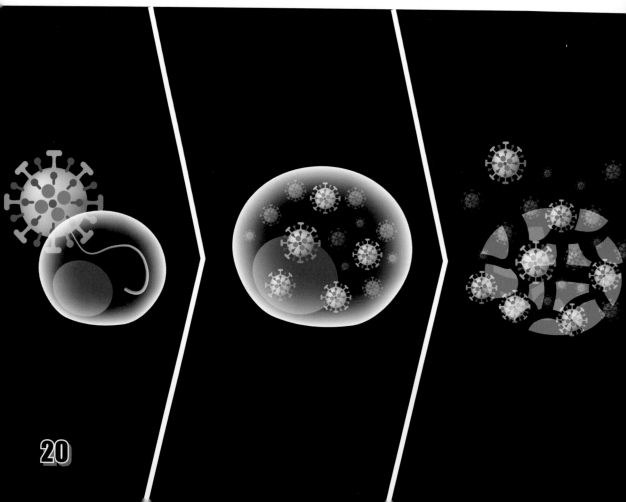

membrane from the inside. This process, called lysis, leads to the death of the host cell.

One strategy used by enveloped viruses is a process called budding. The virus pushes out of the host cell, forming a little bud. It takes some of the cell's membrane as it finally leaves. Some viruses also take a new envelope from other cell structures, such as the nucleus, before transporting outside. Budding doesn't always kill the host cell. Instead, the cell continues to slowly release new viral particles into the outside surroundings.

Most colds are caused by viruses. The best way to fight a cold is to get plenty of rest, drink a lot of water, and eat healthy foods.

FIGHTING VIRUSES

When bacteria make us sick, in many cases, there are medicines called antibiotics we can take to kill them. However, there aren't many antiviral medications we can take after a virus enters our body. This is because bacteria don't use our cells to reproduce the way viruses do. It's hard—but not impossible—to make medications that kill only the virus and not our own cells. People can take medications that relieve the **symptoms** of diseases such as colds and the flu, but these medications don't kill the virus that causes the diseases. The sick person only recovers when the body fights off the virus on its own.

Fast Fact

Coughing and sneezing can spread millions of tiny viruses to other people. This is why people wore masks during parts of the COVID-19 pandemic. It's harder for the virus to get through the fabric of the mask, so there's less chance of someone spreading the disease.

Training the Body

Instead of antiviral medications, our best defense against viruses is vaccination. This is when a weakened virus or part of a virus is injected into the body

THE COVID-19 VACCINE

In the past, vaccines for deadly diseases were made with weaker versions, or types, of the dangerous virus. Over time, scientists realized they could make better vaccines by using only parts of the virus, such as the capsid. Without the whole virus, the person can't be infected, but the immune system can still "see" and destroy those parts when they encounter them again.

This is how the COVID-19 vaccine was made and why it's so safe. Only the outer capsid is in the vaccine. This lets the immune system recognize its spike proteins. When the real virus enters the body, the immune system knows what to do about those spike proteins and can fight it off quickly.

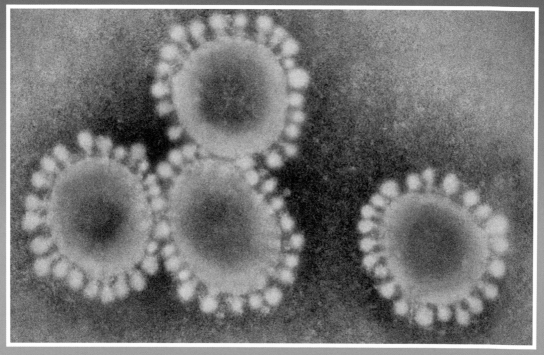

This picture shows SARS-CoV-2, the virus that causes COVID-19, under a microscope. The spike proteins around the outside are clearly visible.

to teach the immune system how to fight it. White blood cells create proteins called antibodies that can attach to a viral capsid or envelope, which prevents the virus from entering and infecting any cells. If the real virus enters the body later, the immune system remembers what it was taught and fights off the virus. Sometimes this happens before you even have a chance to get sick. Other times, it makes the sickness much easier for the body to deal with.

Vaccines have helped keep people safe from deadly diseases for many years, and new ones are being created all the time. For

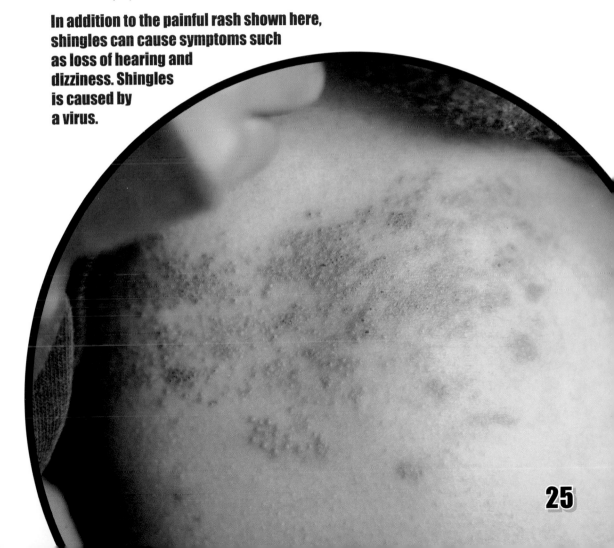

In addition to the painful rash shown here, shingles can cause symptoms such as loss of hearing and dizziness. Shingles is caused by a virus.

example, the varicella-zoster virus can cause two different diseases: chickenpox and shingles. Since 1995, most school-age children receive a vaccination against the varicella-zoster virus to prevent chickenpox.

Chickenpox is a disease marked by itchy blisters covering the whole body. It's normally a mild disease among young children, but it can be very serious for older adults who catch it. In many cases, chickenpox goes away by itself, but the varicella-zoster virus can sometimes hide inside nerve cells. The virus can become active again later and cause shingles, which is a painful, burning rash on the skin.

Continuing to Learn

We have learned a lot about viruses and how they work over the past century, but there's still much more to learn. Unfortunately, new viruses are appearing every year.

Understanding how viruses work not only helps us fight infections; it can help fight some cancers as well. Some viruses cause cancer, but others may be able to help fight cancer. Because viruses can kill cells when they exit, scientists are experimenting with giving cancer patients a virus that targets and kills only their cancer cells.

The virus would not make the cancer patient sick. As of 2022, this field of cancer treatment is being studied to see how well it works. Other kinds of research into viruses, such as the development of new vaccines, is also ongoing.

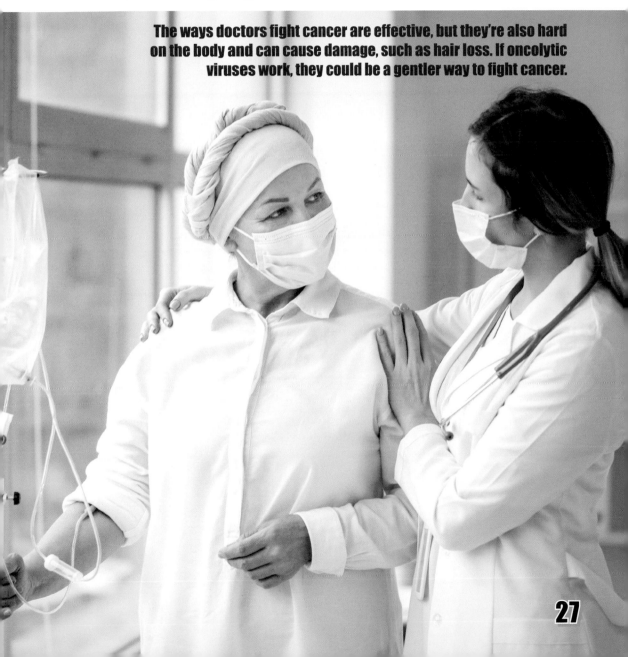

The ways doctors fight cancer are effective, but they're also hard on the body and can cause damage, such as hair loss. If oncolytic viruses work, they could be a gentler way to fight cancer.

THINK ABOUT IT!

1. What ways can you think of to fight germs?

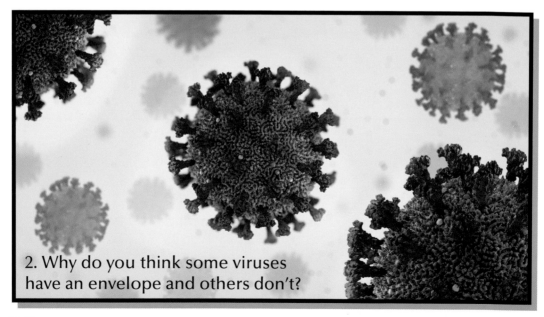

2. Why do you think some viruses have an envelope and others don't?

3. Do you think viruses should be considered alive or not?

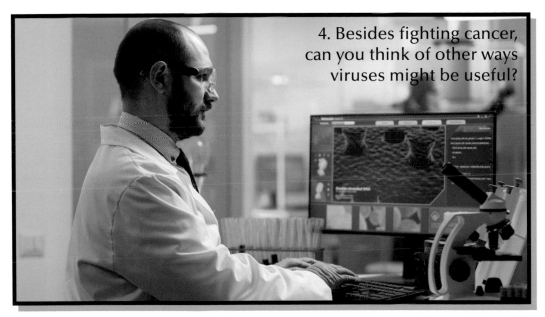

4. Besides fighting cancer, can you think of other ways viruses might be useful?

GLOSSARY

germ: A microscopic thing that causes disease.

infectious: Able to be spread from person to person.

lipid: A type of chemical that doesn't mix well with water. Lipids include fats and cholesterol.

mosaic: A decoration on a surface made by setting small pieces of glass, tile, or stone of different colors into another material so as to make pictures or patterns; something resembling such patterns, especially a virus disease of plants characterized by mottling of the foliage.

nucleic acid: A substance present in living cells and viruses that has molecules consisting of many nucleotides linked in a long chain. DNA and RNA are nucleic acids.

nucleotide: A compound that forms the basic unit of nucleic acid.

parasite: Something that lives in, on, or with another living thing and obtains benefits while harming the host.

proteins: Long chains of molecules called amino acids that are needed to keep living things alive.

sterilize: To free of microscopic living things, especially germs.

symptom: A change in a living thing that indicates the presence of a disease or other physical disorder.

transcription: The process of forming a messenger RNA molecule using a DNA molecule as a guide.

Books

Mayer, Melissa. *The Micro World of Viruses and Bacteria*. North Mankato, MN: Capstone Press, 2022.

Sisteré, Mariona Tolosa. *The Secret Life of Viruses: Incredible Science Facts about Germs, Vaccines, and What You Can Do to Stay Healthy*. Naperville, IL: Sourcebooks eXplore, 2021.

Ter Horst, Marc, and Wendy Panders. *Snot, Sneezes, and Super-spreaders: Everything You Need to Know About Viruses and How to Stop Them*. Vancouver, BC: Greystone Books, 2022.

Websites

BrainPOP: Viruses
www.brainpop.com/health/diseasesinjuriesandconditions/viruses
Watch movies, play games, and take quizzes to learn more about viruses.

Ducksters: Viruses
www.ducksters.com/science/biology/viruses.php
Read more facts about what viruses are and how they spread.

***National Geographic Kids*: Facts about Coronavirus**
kids.nationalgeographic.com/science/article/facts-about-coronavirus
Learn more about the virus that causes COVID-19.

INDEX